Cloud Computing Clusters

FOR

DUMMIES®

AMD SPECIAL EDITION

by Brian Underdahl,
Margaret Lewis, and
Tim Mueting

WILEY

Wiley Publishing, Inc.

Cloud Computing Clusters For Dummies®, AMD Special Edition

Published by
Wiley Publishing, Inc.
111 River Street
Hoboken, NJ 07030-5774
www.wiley.com

Copyright © 2010 by Wiley Publishing, Inc., Indianapolis, Indiana

Published by Wiley Publishing, Inc., Indianapolis, Indiana

ISBN: 978-0-470-64411-9

Manufactured in the United States of America

10 9 8 7 6 5 4 3 2 1

WILEY

Publisher's Acknowledgments

We're proud of this book; please send us your comments through our Dummies online registration form located at http://dummies.custhelp.com. For other comments, please contact our Customer Care Department within the U.S. at 877-762-2974, outside the U.S. at 317-572-3993, or fax 317-572-4002. For details on how to create a custom *For Dummies* book for your business or organization, contact bizdev@wiley.com. For information about licensing the *For Dummies* brand for products or services, contact BrandedRights&Licenses@Wiley.com.

Some of the people who helped bring this book to market include the following:

Acquisitions, Editorial, and Media Development

Project Editor: Jennifer Bingham

Editorial Manager: Rev Mengle

Business Development Representative: Karen Hattan

Custom Publishing Project Specialist: Michael Sullivan

Composition Services

Project Coordinator: Kristie Rees

Layout and Graphics: Samantha K. Cherolis

Proofreader: Jessica Kramer

Publishing and Editorial for Technology Dummies

    Richard Swadley, Vice President and Executive Group Publisher

    Andy Cummings, Vice President and Publisher

    Mary Bednarek, Executive Director, Acquisitions

    Mary C. Corder, Editorial Director

Publishing and Editorial for Consumer Dummies

    Diane Graves Steele, Vice President and Publisher, Consumer Dummies

Composition Services

    Debbie Stailey, Director of Composition Services

Table of Contents

Introduction

*W*elcome to *Cloud Computing Clusters For Dummies,* AMD
Special Edition. You can't read a technology journal or
blog — or even your local newspaper — without coming upon
a reference to cloud computing. Although there's been a lot of
debate about what cloud computing is and where it's headed,
no one has doubts that it is real.

Cloud computing is transforming the computing landscape. It
will change the way technology is deployed and how people
think about the economics of computing. This book provides
a perspective on cloud computing and starts your journey of
exploration.

Cloud computing is more than a service sitting in some remote
data center. It's a set of approaches that can help organizations quickly and effectively add and subtract resources in
almost real time. Unlike other approaches, the cloud is as
much about the business model as it is about technology.
Companies clearly understand that technology is at the heart
of how they operate their businesses. Business executives
have long been frustrated with the complexities of getting
their computing needs met quickly and cost effectively. In a
sense, cloud computing has started to become a mainstream
concept because these business executives have forced the
issue into the forefront.

Cloud Computing Clusters For Dummies, AMD Special Edition
shows you some of the unique ways that AMD is driving the
adoption of cloud computing as an IT infrastructure. The AMD
Opteron™ processors, for example, are especially suited to
cloud server clusters in everything from cost to energy efficiency to virtualization optimization.

About This Book

The term *cloud computing* covers a big area, and comes with a lot of new terms and information. That's what this book discusses. Some people may want to get deeper into the technological details, while others may care only about the business implications.

You can read from cover to cover, but if you're not that kind of person, this book follows the *For Dummies* style of keeping chapters self-contained so you can go straight to the topics that interest you most.

This book was written for, with information supplied by, AMD.

Icons Used in This Book

Throughout the book, you may notice several handy little icons in the margins. They point you to particular types of information:

You may be sorry if this little tidbit slips your mind.

This is a particularly useful point to pay attention to.

Tidbits for the more technically inclined.

Chapter 1

Cloud Computing Defined

● ●

● ●

*I*n a dynamic economic environment, your company's survival may depend on your ability to focus on core business and adapt quickly. In this chapter, we introduce you to cloud computing — what it is and how it helps companies rethink how they deploy technology.

Why Choose Cloud Now?

What is cloud computing? Cloud computing is the next stage in the evolution of the Internet. The *cloud* in cloud computing provides the means through which everything — from computing power to computing infrastructure and applications, from business processes to personal collaboration — can be delivered as a service wherever and whenever needed (see Figure 1-1).

Economics

Some of the most immediate benefits of cloud-based infrastructure services include the ability to add new infrastructure capacity quickly and at a low cost. Therefore, cloud services allow the business to gain IT resources in a self-service manner, which can help save time and money.

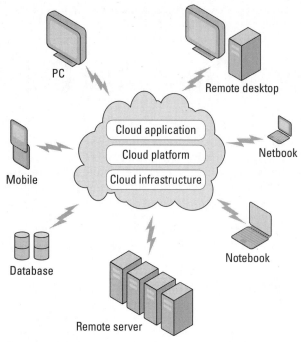

PC

Remote desktop

Cloud application

Cloud platform

Netbook

Cloud infrastructure

Mobile

Database

Notebook

Remote server

Figure 1-1: Ingredients of the cloud.

A typical cloud service provider has *economies of scale* (cost advantages resulting in the ability to spread fixed costs over more customers) that an individual corporation may lack. Moreover, the cloud's self-service capability means that IT departments can tailor the needs of the organization to an IT infrastructure by adding or subtracting *compute cycles* (CPU resources added or subtracted on an incremental basis) or storage as needed.

Virtualization adoption

Any discussion of cloud computing typically begins with virtualization. *Virtualization* is the abstraction of software from hardware. The result is virtual servers or desktops that imitate physical computers. New virtual machines can be rolled out in minutes and running virtual machines can be moved without significantly disrupting the users (if they experience any disruption at all). In short, virtualization provides a high level of IT agility.

Cloud computing and virtualization go hand-in-hand. Like virtualization, cloud computing is an abstraction of IT resources from a physical, defined infrastructure to something that is capable of dynamic change. Cloud computing combines service orientation with distributed manageability and the economies of scale derived from virtualization. In a world where almost everything is a service, virtualization is a fundamental mechanism for delivering services. Without virtualization, the cloud becomes very slow to respond to changes and difficult to manage. Virtualization is important for cloud computing because it makes it possible to simplify and add flexibility to many aspects of IT infrastructure.

Maturity of the technology

For cloud computing to make sense, you need an underlying platform that is proven, efficient, and can grow as needed. The AMD Opteron™ processors have been designed with these considerations in mind — balancing price, performance, and power in a socket design that allows for future upgrades through simple replacement of the processor on the same motherboard.

Understanding Cloud Types

As soon as you start reading about cloud computing, you run into the phrase *as-a-service* an awful lot. Examples include *infrastructure-as-a-service, hardware-as-a-service, social-networks-as-a-service, applications-as-a-service, desktops-as-a-service,* and so on.

The term *service* means a task that has been packaged so it can be automated and delivered to customers in a consistent and repeatable manner. These services may be delivered by a cloud service vendor or through your own internal data center. The three main cloud service delivery models are infrastructure-as-a-service, platform-as-a-service, and software-as-a-service.

Infrastructure-as-a-service – cloud infrastructure

Infrastructure-as-a-service (IaaS) is the delivery of computer hardware (servers, networking technology, storage, and data center space) as a service. It may also include the delivery of operating systems and virtualization technology to manage the resources.

The IaaS customer rents computing resources instead of buying and installing them in his own data center. The service is typically paid for on a usage basis. The service may include *dynamic scaling* so that if the customer winds up needing more resources than expected, he can get them immediately (probably up to a given limit).

Platform-as-a-service – cloud platform

With *platform-as-a-service (PaaS),* the provider delivers more than infrastructure. It delivers what you might call *middleware* — an integrated set of software that provides everything a developer needs to build an application — for both software development and runtime.

PaaS can be viewed as an evolution of Web hosting. In recent years, Web-hosting companies have provided fairly complete software stacks for developing Web sites. PaaS takes this idea a step farther by providing *lifecycle management* — capabilities to manage all software development stages from planning and design, to building and deployment, to testing and maintenance. The primary benefit of PaaS is having software development and deployment capability based entirely in the cloud — hence, the PaaS client need not concern itself too much with management or maintenance efforts.

Software-as-a-service – cloud applications

The most complete implementation of cloud services is *software-as-a-service (SaaS)*. SaaS is an application hosted by the provider and delivered to the user as a service. This includes all the needed hardware and software to run the application and create, manage, and store related data.

SaaS has its roots in an early kind of hosting operation carried out by *application service providers (ASPs)*. Prior to the advent of this type of service, companies often spent huge amounts of money implementing and customizing applications to satisfy internal business requirements. Many of these products were difficult to implement, learn, and use. However, the arrival of social media sites like Facebook and YouTube and free online applications like Gmail demonstrated the success of delivering applications via the Internet to the masses. The lesson learned is that an application delivered as-a-service can be easy to use and easy to stay with.

Defining the Elements of Cloud Computing

The *cloud* itself is a set of hardware, networks, storage, services, and interfaces that enable the delivery of computing-as-a-service. *Cloud services* include the delivery of software, infrastructure, and storage over the Internet (either as separate components or a complete platform) based on user demand.

Taking a cue from the success of social media and online consumer applications, companies are finding some important new value in cloud services. The cloud can eliminate many of the complex constraints from the traditional computing environment, including space, time, power, and cost.

Elasticity and scalability

The service provider can't anticipate how and when users will access the service. One user might use the service three times a year, whereas another might use it daily. A global event might trigger a huge surge of users all trying to access the service at the same time.

Therefore, the service needs to be available all the time and it has to be designed to scale upward for high periods of demand and downward for lighter ones. *Scalability* also means that the cloud infrastructure can absorb additional users without decreasing responsiveness.

This ability to scale is achieved by providing *elasticity*. Think about the rubber band and its properties. If you're holding together a dozen pens with a rubber band, you probably have to fold it in half. However, if you're trying to keep 100 pens together, you will have to stretch that rubber band. How can a single rubber band accomplish both tasks? Simply, it is elastic. So is the cloud.

Self-service provisioning

Users can easily get cloud services without going through a lengthy process. The user simply requests an amount of computing, storage, software, process, or other resources from the service provider.

Contrast this on-demand response with the process at a typical data center: When a department is about to implement a new application, it has to submit a request to the data center for additional computing hardware, software, services, or process resources. The data center gets similar requests from departments across the company and must sort through all requests and evaluate the availability of existing resources versus the need to purchase new hardware.

Application programming interfaces

Cloud services need to have standardized APIs. These interfaces provide the instructions on how two applications or data sources can communicate with each other.

A standardized interface lets the customer more easily link a cloud service, such as a customer relationship management system, with another system like financial accounts management without having to resort to custom programming.

Billing of services

A cloud environment needs a built-in service that bills customers. And, of course, to calculate that bill, usage has to be *metered* (tracked). Even free cloud services (such as Google's Gmail or Zoho's Internet-based office applications) are metered.

Service management

A cloud service provider must include a service management environment. A *service management environment* is an integrated approach for managing your physical environments and IT systems. This environment must be able to maintain the required service level for that organization.

In other words, service management has to monitor and optimize the service or sets of services. Service management has to consider key issues, such as performance of the overall system, including security and performance.

Security

Many customers must take a leap of faith to trust that the cloud service is safe. Turning over critical data or application infrastructure to a cloud-based service provider requires making sure that the information can't be accidentally accessed by another company (or maliciously accessed by a hacker).

Many companies have compliance requirements for securing both internal and external information. Without the right level of security, a company might not be able to use a provider's offerings.

Private versus Public Clouds

Although many business executives are attracted to the idea of the public cloud, just as many are interested in achieving the benefits of the cloud, but on an internal basis. There are different reasons why companies investigating a cloud might want a private cloud instead of using a public one. The most obvious reason is privacy and security of data. And some companies are considering the private cloud because they have already invested in a lot of hardware, software, and space and would like to be able to leverage their investments, but in a more efficient manner.

There's confusion over the definition of a private cloud. When we say *private cloud,* we mean a highly virtualized cloud data center located inside your company's firewall. However, it may also be a private space dedicated to your company within a cloud vendor's data center designed to handle your company's workloads.

A private cloud exhibits the key characteristics of a public cloud, including elasticity, scalability, and self-service provisioning. The major difference is *control* over the environment. In a private cloud, you (or a trusted partner) control the service management.

Chapter 2

The Foundation for Cloud Clusters

· ·

In This Chapter

▶ Transforming the data center

▶ Figuring out the importance of the processor for cloud

▶ Examining virtualization and cloud computing clusters

· ·

*T*his chapter takes a deeper look at some of the technical aspects of clouds. From efficient multi-core processor-based hardware to well-developed virtualization software, the pieces you need are available today. In this chapter, you see what those pieces are and how they fit together as the foundation of cloud clusters.

Changing the Face of the Data Center

The emerging cloud computing model is changing the whole concept of the data center in some very important ways. In this section, we look at how the data center is evolving and some of the factors driving this change (see Figure 2-1).

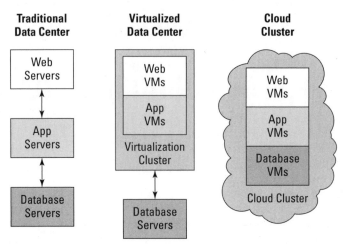

Figure 2-1: How the data center is changing.

The traditional data center

The traditional data center can be summed up as racks of x86 servers running at full power, but maybe less than fully utilized. Each server could be dedicated to one application. The environment can be scaled by adding more servers, which means more floor space, more power, and more cooling. The major reasons why IT is moving away from this hot and heavy data center model are the rising cost of energy and difficulties in managing this sprawling environment.

The virtualized data center

The evolution of the virtualized data center is tied to the rise of the hypervisor in the world of x86 servers. A hypervisor — or virtual machine monitor — is a piece of software that allows multiple operating systems to run on a computer at the same time. In effect, this means that a single computer can appear to be multiple computers (or virtual machines) and several applications can be consolidated on this one server.

Today, hypervisors are being optimized for increased virtual machine density, which can reduce overhead and take advantage of the latest hardware acceleration features.

Hypervisors are also being improved to support better power management, such as *core parking,* which is the ability to consolidate VMs (virtual machines) onto fewer cores and turn off the unneeded cores to save power.

The trend to virtualization means consolidation to fewer servers, which in turn helps to reduce power and cooling. We are in the middle of this move to a higher density and more efficient computing environment, with many big companies having some percentage of their data center already virtualized and many smaller companies jumping on the bandwagon.

The cloud computing data center

The emergence of cloud computing has come with the explosive growth of social media sites and the resulting demands of their very large data centers for hardware platforms with a balanced approached to performance and operational costs.

You could say that virtual machines make the cloud possible, because each physical server in the cloud can serve many different purposes at the same time. In fact, some have said that virtualization of servers is a core foundation of cloud computing.

From a hardware standpoint, multi-core processors have enabled a higher density and more efficient computing environment. Virtualization-optimized hardware continues to reduce the overhead of virtualization software and further improve the density.

In addition, hardware platforms that are optimized to take a balanced approach to power consumption and raw performance are allowing cloud computing environments to scale upwards even as data center power and cooling limits are reached. Features like clock gating, frequency adjusting, core idling, dynamically turning off part of the microprocessor, turning down the frequency to reduce voltage, or shutting down one or more cores can enable the processor to provide the needed performance, while reducing power consumption and heat output.

Why the Processor Matters for Cloud Computing

For a server to be well-suited to cloud computing, it should balance performance, power, and price. Achieving such a balance in an on-demand service environment can be tricky because the service is at the mercy of the user's utilization, which can fluctuate wildly. As such, achieving a balance between performance, power, and price requires an ability to scale and deliver performance, power consumption, memory management, I/O, and throughput.

Server platforms based on the AMD Opteron™ processor can more effectively manage these competing factors because the AMD Opteron processors have been designed with this type of balancing in mind. As such, AMD Opteron processors are excellent choices for cloud computing uses:

- ✔ AMD Opteron processors provide a high level of performance. When it was introduced in 2003, it was the first 64-bit-compatible x86 microprocessor. Moreover, the AMD Opteron processor offered Direct Connect Architecture, which helped lead the transition to 64-bit computing and wider memory addressing. By enabling these transitions, the AMD Opteron processor packed more computing power into the processors, which helped improve both server performance and virtualization-related uses.

- ✔ The AMD Opteron processor has improved performance over time by packing more *cores* — brains, if you will — into the processor. Not only does this give the processor more raw computing power, but it also has the ability to conserve energy by reducing the distance electrical signals have to travel to perform compute functions. Electrical signals that stay within the processor package don't have to travel as far to carry out their tasks, so both speed and energy consumption can be improved.

  The AMD Opteron processor led the way in the transition from single-core to multi-core for x86 processors in 2005, reflecting the ongoing effort to keep dynamically scalable performance resources in place.

Of course, raw compute power isn't the only consideration in terms of achieving balance between performance, power, and price. Ongoing and future costs such as energy expenditures should be considered as well. Controlling future energy costs is something that AMD has long understood. AMD helped pioneer energy-efficient technology, dating back to the original AMD Opteron processor. Today, AMD processors include a suite of power management features called AMD-P (for more on this product, see Chapter 3).

AMD also took the lead in offering ultra-low power processors. A good example is the AMD Opteron 4100 Series processors, which were designed specifically for the dense, low-power environments like Web hosting and cloud computing. The AMD Opteron 4100 Series processors include an ultra-low power (EE) product that has a 35W thermal design power (TDP), offering the lowest power processor capable of supporting both one- and two-socket servers.

TDP is the thermal design power specifications provided to platform designers and industry partners. TDP is primarily used as a guideline for manufacturers of thermal solutions (heatsinks/fans, and so on) that tells them how much heat their solution should dissipate.

Much of the power consumed by a processor is turned into heat, so reducing power consumption helps make the processor run cooler. This reduced heat production provides the additional benefit of reducing the level of cooling needed to control the data center's temperature — saving even more on power costs.

Virtualization and Cloud Computing Clusters

Any discussion of cloud computing typically begins with virtualization. Think of cloud computing as the transformation of computing that brings together service orientation with distributed manageability, all combined with the economies of scale from virtualization. In a world where almost everything is a service, virtualization is a fundamental mechanism for delivering services. Indeed, virtualization provides a platform for optimizing complex IT resources in a *scalable* manner, which is ideal for delivering services.

Characteristics of virtualization

Virtualization has three characteristics that make it ideal for cloud computing:

- ✔ **Partitioning:** In virtualization, many applications and operating systems (OSes) are supported in a single physical system by *partitioning* (separating) the available resources.

- ✔ **Isolation:** Each virtual machine is isolated from its host physical system and other virtualized machines. Because of this isolation, if one virtual machine crashes, it doesn't affect the other virtual machines. In addition, data may not be shared between one virtual container and another.

- ✔ **Encapsulation:** A virtual machine can be represented (and even stored) as a single file, so you can identify it easily based on the service it provides. In essence, the encapsulated process could be a business service. This encapsulated virtual machine can be presented to an application as a complete entity. Therefore, encapsulation can protect each application so that it doesn't interfere with another application.

Hardware-assisted virtualization

A *hypervisor* is an operating system, which means that it knows how to act as a traffic cop to make things happen in an orderly manner. The hypervisor sits at the lowest levels of the hardware environment.

Because in cloud computing, you need to support many different operating environments, the hypervisor becomes an ideal delivery mechanism. The hypervisor lets you show the same application on lots of systems without having to physically copy that application onto each system. One twist: Because of the hypervisor architecture, it can load any different operating system as though it were just another application. Therefore, the hypervisor is a very practical way of getting things virtualized quickly and efficiently.

Virtualization is memory-intensive software that puts a lot of demands on a server. It depends on a close working relationship between hardware and software to keep complexity and overhead as minimal as possible. AMD, of course, fully supports virtualization through AMD Virtualization™ (AMD-V™) technology, a set of hardware extensions designed to help simplify virtualization solutions. For a list of features associated with AMD-V, see Table 2-1.

Table 2-1   AMD-V Technology Features

Feature	Benefits
Virtualization extensions to the x86 instruction set	Enables software to more efficiently create virtual machines so that multiple operating systems and their applications can run simultaneously on the same computer.
Tagged TLB	Hardware features that facilitate efficient switching between virtual machines for better application responsiveness.
Rapid Virtualization Indexing (RVI)	Helps accelerate the performance of many virtualized applications by enabling hardware-based virtual machine memory management.
AMD Extended Migration	Hardware feature that helps virtualization software enable live migration of virtual machines between all available AMD Opteron processor generations.
I/O Virtualization	Enables direct device access by a virtual machine, bypassing the hypervisor for improved application performance and improved isolation of virtual machines for increased integrity and security.

Leveraging virtualization

As the IT world gains familiarity with virtualization technology and as the technology matures, organizations are leveraging virtualization to solve far more than their server consolidation challenges. Increasingly, customers are using virtualization for disaster recovery, high availability, remote clients, and ultimately, managing the delivery of business applications to end-users. This next generation of virtualization offers new levels of automation and orchestration in the data center that extend beyond servers to include the network and storage.

Chapter 3

The Anatomy of Cloud Servers

*T*he cloud can't exist without the proper servers. Just as it is important to choose a vehicle that meets the needs and requirements of your family, you need the correct servers if you want to successfully provide cloud services. A bargain PC from your local electronics store isn't going to suit a cloud computing center any better than a two-seat sports car will do much for a family with several young children — even if there is a lot to be said for some two-seat sports cars!

If you want to build a solid foundation for cloud computing, you need to adopt systems with the right balance of processing horsepower and energy efficiency. Increasingly, building that solid foundation also means consolidating servers via virtualization in order to boost utilization levels and cut maintenance costs. Of course, a cloud environment must ultimately fit your budget, too, so making the correct choices is very important.

In this chapter, we look at some of the important choices you must make in order to put together the set of cloud servers that will suit the needs of your customers.

Scalability

Scalability is the ability of a system to handle different amounts of work in a graceful manner. For cloud computing, this means being able to achieve economies of scale by managing a very large pool of computing resources in a highly economic and efficient fashion.

How do you manage the computing resources in the cloud? One basic requirement is that workloads need to be organized. A *workload* is an independent service or collection of code that can be executed. A workload can be a small or complete application.

You must be able to balance two things:

- The applications or components running in the cloud
- The needs of the business to perform predictably, especially during peak loads

Essential components of any cloud computing environment are servers equipped with processors that deliver excellent performance, strong I/O characteristics, low energy consumption, and robust virtualization assistance. AMD Opteron™ processors offer all these qualities while also providing scalability.

For example, the AMD Opteron 4100 Series processors are for those customers seeking an economical, power-efficient server solution in a 1P and 2P configuration. The AMD Opteron 6100 Series processors are for customers seeking even more processing power — they offer 16 to 48 cores with a large memory footprint in 2P and 4P configurations. These platforms can be customizable in terms of sockets, chipsets, cores, and thermal bands, and therefore can be used as the basis for simple infrastructure servers or finely tuned and architected solutions capable of handling dense and scalable computing environments (for example, high performance computing [HPC] and cloud computing).

AMD Opteron processor-based servers offer the following benefits of a scalable solution:

- ✔ They enable customized solutions, which may be required by large cloud providers.

- ✔ They come in standard, low power (HE), and ultra-low power (EE) versions to enable you to match workload and power requirements to your specific energy constraints.

- ✔ They offer a consistent feature set across all products regardless of power bands, chipsets, frequency, or number of cores.

- ✔ They provide a common architecture for ease of management and flexibility spanning both AMD Opteron 4000 and 6000 Series platforms.

- ✔ They are designed to accommodate single, dual, and quad socket servers, which enables server scalability from 4 to 48 cores per server platform.

I/O Throughput

No matter how fast and powerful a processor may be, it may not be very useful if it can't communicate with the outside world. That's why I/O (input/output) performance, also known as I/O throughput, is so important.

I/O throughput is even more important in cloud computing environments than it might be in some other computing arenas because of the remote nature of cloud computing. When virtually all processing is done at a distance, it is especially important to reduce any delays so that the end-user won't get the feeling that the cloud is slow, unresponsive, or sluggish — they can go to the DMV office if they want that kind of treatment!

AMD Opteron processors use HyperTransport™ technology to increase communication speeds with the outside world. HyperTransport technology is a high-speed, low-latency, point-to-point link designed to increase the communication speed between integrated circuits in computers, servers, embedded systems, and networking and telecommunications equipment.

HyperTransport Technology was invented at AMD with contributions from some of their industry partners. The technology helps reduce the number of buses in a system, which can reduce system bottlenecks and use system memory more efficiently in high-end multiprocessor systems.

Power Efficiency

Imagine for a moment that you were personally responsible for the gas bill for a taxi company with hundreds of big, gas-hog taxis sitting idle while waiting for fares. You'd probably be pretty interested in finding ways to make the fleet more efficient. You might, for example, want to have the drivers shut off their engines while they're just sitting by the curb or you might want to switch to smaller, more fuel-efficient vehicles.

In many ways, a cloud computing server center is similar to that taxi fleet because even though each processor uses just a little energy, when you add up the energy demands of a whole server farm, the usage totals can be staggering. Anything you can do to save a little energy here and some more over there helps the bottom line.

The unique demands of Web hosting and cloud computing can result in power efficiency being as important as, if not more important than, raw performance, and AMD's energy efficient processors are perfectly suited for this kind of task. AMD's energy efficient processors deliver a high power profile while still maintaining acceptable performance for these types of workloads.

AMD is doing its part to reduce the power consumption while delivering real-world performance and a full set of features. AMD Opteron processors come with the AMD-P suite of power management capabilities that dynamically minimizes power usage of the overall processor, individual cores, and the logic within each core, based on application needs and server workloads. For more info on AMD-P, see Table 3-1.

Table 3-1	The AMD-P Suite of Power Management Capabilities
Capability	*Benefit*
AMD CoolCore™ Technology	Can reduce energy consumption by turning off unused parts of the processor.
AMD Smart Fetch Technology	Helps reduce power consumption by allowing idle cores to enter a "halt" state, causing them to draw even less power during processing idle times, without compromising system performance.
Independent Dynamic Core Technology	Enables variable clock frequency for each core, depending on the specific performance requirement of the applications it is supporting, helping to reduce power consumption.
Dual Dynamic Power Management (DDPM) Technology	Provides an independent power supply to the cores and to the memory controller, allowing the cores and memory controller to operate on different voltages, depending on usage.
AMD PowerCap manager	Provides the ability to put a cap on the P-state level of a core via the BIOS, helping to deliver consistent, predictable power consumption of a system.
AMD C1E	Enables unused cores to be turned off to provide enhanced power savings during system idle times.

AMD-P enables the processor to provide the needed performance while reducing power consumption, which in turn produces less heat. Therefore, AMD-P technologies help control costs on two fronts: direct power consumption by the processors, and indirect power consumption required to deal with the heat thrown off by those processors.

Together, those technologies can help enable cutting-edge energy efficiency. That can be a major competitive advantage for cloud service providers, whose data centers typically house large volumes of power-hungry servers.

A Balanced Approach to Performance, Power, and Price

The servers in your cloud computing center really need to deliver optimal performance and price, if they're going to fill the bill. You need servers that are matched to the job. Servers based on AMD Opteron processors, designed to meet the needs of cloud computing, can be the answer.

AMD's Opteron processors simplify cloud server management tasks. The 4100 and 6100 Series use the same BIOS base code, the same programming interface, similar drivers, AMD Virtualization™ (AMD-V™) technology, and the AMD-P suite of power management features. The AMD Extended Migration functionality enables live migration of virtual machines across all available AMD Opteron processor generations. This functionality can help cloud service providers manage vast virtual server farms without incurring downtime. All these features combine to make the AMD Opteron processors a great choice for cloud servers.

The AMD Opteron™ 4100 Series processors

Targeted for specialized workloads like Web hosting and cloud computing, the AMD Opteron 4100 Series processors offer a choice of single or dual sockets with either four or six cores, all within the same scalable infrastructure. The AMD 4100 Series processors includes standard, low power (HE), and ultra-low power (EE) products to match workload and power requirements for today's cloud computing environments.

The AMD Opteron 4100 Series EE processors are intended to operate at lower idle power than the higher performing models. In this type of environment, saving just a few watts of power per server is a big deal because the power savings ripple throughout the rest of the system. These processors also produce less heat, which means that you can reduce fan capacity, and use smaller and more efficient power supplies.

These processors, at 35W TDP versus 40W TDP, are the lowest-power processors available capable of supporting both 1P and 2P server configurations in the industry, with no feature compromises — each processor offers a consistent feature set for ease of management and flexibility.

The AMD Opteron 4000 Series platforms offer outstanding performance-per-watt to align the performance needs with power and budget realities.

The AMD Opteron™ 6100 Series processors

The AMD Opteron 6000 Series platform is the server platform you can count on as real-world workloads become increasingly complex and demanding. Based on the next-generation AMD Direct Connect Architecture 2.0 with up to 48 total cores in a 4P configuration, this platform can greatly increase the memory bandwidth to amounts that outpace previous-generation 2P and 4P servers. These specifications can help your business tackle complex jobs with greater throughput, exceptional value, and readiness to scale.

In addition, you can gain a distinct advantage normally reserved for high-end systems with exceptional value, low total cost of ownership, and generational consistency. Tackle virtualization and database and infrastructure workloads cost effectively, with configurations offering high performance at low cost.

The AMD Opteron 6000 Series platforms offer an outstanding performance and scalability for memory and data intensive workloads.

Chipsets that work with you

Other semiconductor components critical to enabling cloud computing are the core logic chipset and memory. The processor and the chipset really are partners and must be designed to work together. Here, AMD has delivered its own chipset, the AMD SR56x0 chipset, which integrates chipset-resident functions into its AMD Opteron processor-based platforms and is enabled with I/O virtualization technology (IOMMU) for these memory- and I/O-intensive environments. There are also low power versions of these chipsets, which can increase the energy efficiency of your infrastructure by consuming less energy and producing less heat.

Chapter 4

Accessing the Cloud

· ·

In This Chapter

▶ Examining clients in cloud computing

▶ Moving desktops to the cloud

▶ Looking at desktop as a service

▶ Understanding AMD's offerings in hardware

▶ Reviewing some use cases

▶ Managing desktops in the cloud

· ·

*T*oday, local computing on the client is the norm, offering a predictable user experience and the flexibility to run different applications. However, the basic concept of cloud computing is access via the Internet anytime, anywhere, with any device. This means the cloud computing cluster has to be able to deliver applications, data, and a satisfying user experience to a wide range of client devices. This chapter takes a closer look at the role of clients in cloud computing.

The Role of Clients in Cloud Computing

Cloud computing clusters can be divided into three general types of clouds: professional clouds, personal clouds and performance clouds (see Figure 4-1). Each of these clouds provides applications, data, and services to users who access these clouds with a variety of client devices.

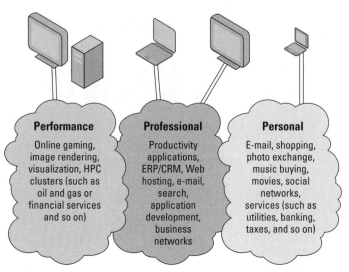

Figure 4-1: Cloud computing use cases.

Professional clouds

Professional clouds provide services to commercial business, government, or educational organizations. E-mail, business applications, and databases are all moving to the cloud in some form or fashion. The professional cloud needs to be able to integrate workstations, desktop PCs, regular and ultra-light notebooks, thin clients, and other devices with hosted servers, data, and services. Users' desktop data can be secured in the cloud, IT management simplified, and centralized, and IT expenditures reduced. For these reasons, there is lot of interest in exploring the cost-effectiveness of cloud-based desktops.

AMD is uniquely suited to meet the needs of these professional cloud users with VISION Pro Technology from AMD, which provides commercial desktops and notebooks with enhanced visual clarity, vibrant colors, and support for seamless multi-monitor functionality. VISION Pro Technology is an advanced visual platform with multi-core processing power to spare for today's and tomorrow's business applications, both on and off the cloud.

Personal clouds

Personal clouds support our personal lives and include things like online banking, utilities, shopping, entertainment, and accessing social media sites. Users want anytime access to data and applications, and they don't really care about the technology infrastructure of the cloud that supports them. According to a Pew Research Center study conducted in 2008, roughly 69 percent of online Americans use Web mail services, store data online, or use software programs whose functionality is located on the Web. As with the professional cloud, the devices used to access these personal clouds are a broad range of clients including desktops, all-in-one computers, and notebooks of all sizes.

Performance clouds

Performance clouds focus on delivering computationally and graphics intensive applications. This emerging type of cloud can deliver high performance computing applications, including video games and other graphically-intensive applications over the Internet. For the consumer, the performance cloud needs to stream visually rich content to virtually any type of mobile device with a Web browser without making the device rapidly deplete battery life or struggle to process the content.

AMD is well positioned for driving the performance cloud, because they're the only hardware provider in the industry designing and delivering both high-performance CPU and GPU technologies (at least as of the time this went to print). AMD is merging this technology to create the Accelerated Processing Unit (APU), which combines general-purpose x86 CPU cores with programmable vector processing engines on a single silicon die.

VISION Pro Technology also delivers a new way to help consumers select the PC that best meets their needs. Rather than the traditional model, which focuses on the technical specifications of individual hardware components, VISION Pro Technology communicates the value of the whole system and demonstrates the combined processing power of both the CPU and GPU to deliver a superior visual experience to mainstream PC users. VISION Pro Technology emphasizes how an AMD-based PC is optimized for video, digital media, and content creation activities.

Moving Desktops to the Cloud

Over the past few years, the notion of a virtual desktop has been getting a lot of attention. With a *virtual desktop,* the PC doesn't run its own applications — they run on a server in a data center. Sound sort of familiar?

Why is it attractive? Think about a PC's *total cost of ownership (TCO):* acquisition, maintenance, support, help desk, hardware, software, and power. In a typical enterprise situation, the annual support cost per PC is anywhere between three and five times the cost of the PC itself. Another thing that drives up the TCO is the fact that PCs need to be replaced approximately every four years.

Across industries

Virtualization is popular in a number of industries. For example, in healthcare, clinicians are using a virtualized desktop to gain access to information in any patient room or office. In science labs, where space is at a premium and contaminant-free work areas are a priority, virtualized desktops eliminate the server and other hardware from the room.

The client desktop

Virtualizing the client desktop can happen four ways, each of which is described in the following sections. You could loosely describe every one of these techniques as *client virtualization,* because in each technique the PC is controlled from the data center (not from the desktop). In practice, however, only one of these techniques, VDI, is based on *true* virtualization, which is the use of software to emulate a computing environment within another computer.

Session-based computing

In *session-based computing,* the user is really running a session on a server. The server is running a single instance of the Windows operating system with multiple sessions. Only the screen image is actually transmitted to the user, who may have a thin client or possibly an old PC.

Operating-system streaming

In *operating-system streaming,* the Windows OS software is passed to the client device — but only as much of the software that's needed at any point in time. Technically, this process is called *streaming.*

Virtual desktop infrastructure

Here, *virtual PCs* (complete emulations of a PC) are created on the server. The user has what *appears* on the server to be a complete PC. The graphics are being sent to a desktop. Today, most people refer to this kind of client virtualization as *virtual desktop infrastructure (VDI).*

The PC blade

A *server blade* is a server computer contained entirely on a single computer board that can be slotted into a *blade cabinet* — a purpose-built computer cabinet with a built-in power supply. The server blade can contain a number of PC blades.

Desktop-as-a-Service

You get two big advantages to moving desktops to the cloud:

✔ **You can create desktops at your own speed.** You might first virtualize your desktops, wherever they are, and replace them with thin clients. The PC blades or VDI servers (or whatever the provider uses to house your virtual desktops) are located at the provider's data center. You generally pay the provider a fee for this.

✔ **You can get as many resources as you need for these desktops.** And, if the HR department needs more resources, the cloud provider has them ready, as well. Say you have offices in New York and Hong Kong: When the New York office is dark and everyone is asleep, you can use the same resources for Hong Kong because of the virtualization on the back end.

How can you deploy and manage these desktops? What is your window into this process? *Desktop-as-a-service* or *DaaS* removes a layer of complexity associated with deploying and managing VDI.

The provider takes the entire virtualization technology infrastructure and unifies it with a management front end that enables your IT to provision these desktops and monitor resource usage. Of course, this idea works as well in a public cloud as it does in a private cloud.

What's the difference between desktop virtualization that runs in your data center and desktop virtualization that runs in a cloud? The technology is basically the same. However, the data center usually supports lots of *workloads* (different applications with lots of different operating systems and middleware) with different requirements and much less automation. A cloud, on the other hand, is optimized for more specialized and fewer workloads and therefore can be easier to automate. Chances are you won't run an application that only services 50 people in a cloud environment. Leave that for the data center.

AMD and the Role of Hardware

The core pieces of any cloud computing environment, regardless of the architecture, are servers equipped with processors that balance performance, energy efficiency, and a robust virtualization feature set. The same holds true for hosting desktops in the cloud. The AMD Opteron™ processors are designed with the features needed to support the performance and isolation requirements of the virtualization and power efficiency technology, like AMD-V™ and AMD-P, used in cloud computing and hosted desktop architectures like VDI, Blade PCs, and OS and application streaming implementations.

Use Cases for Hosted Desktops

Hosted desktops enable a user to run any existing off-the-shelf or custom application without modification. The hosted desktop model works well for unique desktops or applications that have unusual system requirements; for example, older applications that would need to be rewritten or that simply don't run in other server-based computing (SBC) environments can be run as-is.

Hosted desktops can enhance a company's disaster recovery (DR) plan. In the case of a disaster, be it natural or electronic, secure and continued access to the organization's desktop environments is critical to reduce disruption. Virtualized hosted desktops can be easily moved or redeployed to ensure quick recovery and business continuity.

Today's highly mobile workforce demands corporate data access from remote locations. Hosted desktops enable employees using mobile devices to securely access their desktops, along with their authorized applications and associated data, with the ability to protect corporate assets if their devices are lost or stolen.

A hosted desktop also bridges the gap between the users' desire to have a personalized, isolated desktop experience and the IT administrators' need to maintain a secure, centrally controlled and managed computing environment. Outsourced or offshore activities (call center operations, order and back-office processing, or software development, for example) can be managed and maintained within the secure confines of the corporate data center, and users still have their own desktop environments. IT administrators can grant users controlled access to confidential information and intellectual property, while also protecting sensitive information.

Advantages of Desktops in the Cloud

With a hosted desktop implementation, each user gets a unique environment. Each of these environments can be completely customized with different applications and settings without impacting other users. Thus, users can be granted more control of their own virtual desktops, allowing them to install and modify applications if needed.

Moreover, the hosted desktop model makes it possible to consolidate enterprise desktops. IT administrators may be able to replace computer workstations with expendable, low-cost, thin client terminals, which may help to extend computer life cycles because older computers can be repurposed for other duties.

Desktops can be managed centrally, simplifying desktop installations, backups, and maintenance, and reducing technical support and administration. And because user desktops — including operating system images — are running on servers within the walls of a centralized data center, data can be made more secure.

In a virtual desktop infrastructure (VDI) model, the user desktop is decoupled from specific hardware resources, enabling live migration of desktops between physical servers. Alternately, a VM (desktop) can be suspended: The server can move the memory contents of the desktop VM to a disk, a VM can be provisioned on another physical piece of hardware (that is, a server), and the VM can then be brought back online.

After this VDI operation is completed, users can pick up right where they left off. It is also possible to have a session time out after a certain amount of time. The user's session can be disconnected from the client (still running on the server), and the system can then suspend the session by moving the memory contents to disk and freeing up the hardware for another user. When the first user logs back in, the session is reconnected and the user can continue work — regardless of how long it has been since they were disconnected.

Managing desktops in the cloud

From a management perspective, you should understand that cloud desktop virtualization doesn't remove the need for management at the desktop. Additionally, you may still need to manage laptops and PCs that can't be virtualized, and that task may still place a heavy demand on support.

In terms of managing desktops in the cloud, you need to monitor at least two *key performance indicators (KPIs)* regardless of the model you choose:

- ✔ **Annual support costs per device:** This metric is preferable to the total cost of ownership, which includes variable uncontrollable costs such as software licenses and device purchases.

- ✔ **Availability:** This metric, which measures uptime, should be close to 100 percent with virtualized cloud desktops.

The reality for most organizations is that the client environment is managed quite separately from the data center, and may even have its own support staff. For efficiency reasons — and because the technology to enable it is improving fast — the management of the two domains will likely become more integrated in coming years — especially given this cloud model.

Keeping track of your assets in the cloud

Even if your desktops move to the cloud, you're still responsible for keeping track of your assets, as well as monitoring how your services are running.

In fact, you need to track at least five areas whatever your cloud model:

- ✔ **Asset management:** No matter what the client environment is (cell phone, BlackBerry, thin client, and so on), activities within that container need to be registered, monitored, and tracked, based on the hardware itself, the software that runs on the platform, and how various groups use it.

- ✔ **Service monitoring:** Activities in this process area monitor what's happening at each client, as well as the tasks required to maintain the right level of service. The service desk provides coordination for monitoring.

- ✔ **Change management:** Activities in this process area involve managing and implementing all changes in applications and hardware. Although you may often be working off a golden image, management is still important.

  A *golden image* means that every user will have the identical environment. If something goes wrong, an administrator simply gives that user a new copy of the same image so less management is needed for each individual desktop user.

- ✔ **Security:** Activities in this process area involve securing the whole client domain against external threats and authenticating which users can get into which facilities.

✔ **Governance:** Cloud services need to be considered in connection with your governance strategy and your ability to comply with industry and government regulations (like Sarbanes-Oxley, Health Insurance Portability and Accountability Act, and Payment Card Industry Security Standards). For example, desktops in the cloud allow for all types of data to pass through and be stored. You need a plan to ensure continued compliance with regulations.

Chapter 5

Top Ten Cool Examples of Cloud Computing

*C*loud computing really can be a lot of different things, so it's kind of hard to make up a list of the ten coolest examples of cloud computing. Still, *For Dummies* books have a tradition of trying to do such a list, if for no better reason than to get you thinking about the possibilities. So here goes with our list of interesting examples of cloud computing:

✔ Somewhere around 20 hours worth of video are uploaded to YouTube every minute. We guess that means you'll never catch up because that's almost three years of video content added every day!

✔ Almost 1,000 photos are uploaded to Facebook every second. That's about 86 million a day, or about 85.99 million you'll never see.

✔ Some estimates say that there are currently over 100 million minutes of Internet-based video calls made every day. How many of them are telemarketers calling during dinner?

✔ You can use Google Apps to securely store and work on data in XLS, DOC, PPT, and PDF compatible formats from any computer that has Internet access, even if that computer lacks the programs that can open those documents locally. Now it's even easier to put on a slideshow that will put your audience to sleep.

✔ Sales people can deliver rich media presentations using Internet hosted content viewed on the client's choice of displays. And cloud-based content can be quickly adapted for different audiences or to provide answers to unanticipated questions.

✔ Using services from companies like 3tera, you can build cloud-based applications simply by choosing different components from a visual set of building blocks. It's almost like playing with Lego blocks but without worrying about losing a bunch of little pieces in the rug.

✔ Online backup services use the cloud to make it possible to easily store copies of your important data offsite. You might even say that cloud-based backup is the ultimate in offsite backup because no one really knows where the offsite site is.

✔ If you want to buy or sell something online without a lot of payment hassles, you might use a service like Google Checkout or PayPal. With these, you can instantly send money almost anywhere and they'll even conveniently withdraw the funds directly from your bank account in the blink of an eye.

✔ With Google Earth, you can visit almost any place on the planet and view pictures, comments, and suggestions that other users have linked to those locations. Now there's no reason to wonder if Joe's Fresh Seafood Shack is really the place you want to stop for lunch or if it might be wiser to start your diet a little early.

✔ Finally, by using cloud computing you can avoid bringing along your laptop and working on your next cross-country flight. After all, although you might be in the clouds, you probably won't be connected to the cloud while you're in flight — just avoid booking a flight that offers Internet access.

Notes

Notes

Notes

Notes